The
Big Noodle

⇥ **Dominie Press, Inc.**

"Noodles are good for us,"
said Mr. Munch to Mrs. Munch.
"We will make a big noodle."

3

They made a big noodle.

They cooked it in a pot.

Mrs. Munch ate one end.

Mr. Munch ate the other end.

When some of the noodle
was gone, they said, "Mmm!"

"This noodle is good!"

When more of the noodle
was gone, they said, "Mmm!"

"This noodle is very good!"

When most of the noodle
was gone, they said, "Mmm!"

"This noodle is very, very good!"

When the noodle
was all gone,
they had a kiss.

Mr. and Mrs. Munch said,
"Noodles are good for us."

"We will make
another big noodle."